THE PASSIONATE LIVES & LEADERS SERIES

James R. Lucas & Phil Hotsenpiller

THE THINKING PRINCIPLE:
USING PASSION TO INNOVATE AND
CREATE VALUE

Quintessential
Books

READ BOLDLY. THINK DEEPLY. LIVE PASSIONATELY.

www.quintessentialbooks.com

BOSTON · KANSAS CITY

Printed In The United States Of America
ISBN 978-0-9823161-2-2

Cover & Layout Design by Barberhaus Design Studios
Cover Design by Jonas Barber
Layout Design by JV Kennedy

Author Photo Of James R. Lucas Copyright © 2006
By Decloud Studio. All Rights Are Reserved. Used By Permission.

Author Photo Of Phil Hotsenpiller Copyright © 2008
By Barry Morgenstein Studios. All Rights Are Reserved. Used By Permission.

*Quintessential
Books*

READ BOLDLY. THINK DEEPLY. LIVE PASSIONATELY.

Visit Quintessential Books At www.quintessentialbooks.com
For More About Passionate Lives And Leaders, Visit www.livesandleaders.com

TABLE OF CONTENTS

THE *THINKING ORGANIZATION*™

Aren't all organizations *"thinking organizations"*?

In a sense, of course, they are. Leaders and people and teams think about things all the time. But if thinking is done without clear purpose and design, that thinking can meander, flounder, contradict other thinking, and negate innovative thought.

Here's the good news: you can design and build a *Thinking Organization*™.

The other news: you can't have one on the cheap. You didn't personally get smart on the cheap, and your organization won't either. In fact, the organization has a huge problem to overcome that you didn't have. You only had to optimize your own thinking, already a prodigious task given your mind's complexity and how much there is to know. But a *Thinking Organization*™ has to optimize *everyone's* thinking, and it has to accomplish this task both individually and collectively.

> WE DON'T JUST NEED PEOPLE WITH BETTER "CRITICAL THINKING" SKILLS OR ANY OTHER KIND OF "THINKING" SKILLS. WE NEED A *THINKING ORGANIZATION*™.

THE THINKING PRINCIPLE

The collective IQ of most organizations is…not brilliant.

The problem is not a shortage of smart people. Few organizations deliberately hire morons, and a high percentage of organizations go out of their way to find the "best and brightest." So the difficulty isn't generally with the raw material (although there are plenty of unthinking people out there who will block our organization's neural pathways if we let them).

There *is* a serious lack of intelligent thought in most organizations, but as quality expert Edwards Deming observed, 85 percent of this problem is systemic and only 15 percent is the product of individual human stupidity and ignorance or mental laziness.

For example, as we write, General Motors—a flagship of the U. S. economy for the better part of a century—has two very clear attributes: 1) a team loaded with really smart, highly educated, well-traveled, experienced, serious, committed people; and 2) a nearly unbroken 30-year track record of declining market share, marketing misses, overemphasis on a few products at the expense of the future, and internal warfare with its own workers. It is an unthinking organization. On paper it shouldn't be, but on the ground it really is.

Thinking Organizations™ say, "Let's maximize the collective intelligence of *all* of our people, regardless of their personal intelligence level or education or experience. We want $1 + 1 + 1$ to equal 5 or 10, not the 1 or 2 that most cultural designs yield (and the 0 that some generate). We know that thinking isn't an event. It's a way of life. Let's embed collaborative and mutually reinforcing thinking into our cultural design. Let's build the keys to effective thinking into the way we think and then talk about the real-life realities, opportunities, and opportunities disguised as disasters that come our way."

Thinking well collectively can only happen by design—not organizational or structural design, but *cultural* design. If we want to become a *Thinking Organization*™, if we want to have a high level of *Thinking Capital*™, then we have to build thinking into the biology of our organizations. We have to code it into our cultural DNA. And we have to have the thinking infrastructure to move our formal leaders and people collectively toward powerhouse thinking and the results that flow from it.

Thinking *can* be designed and built into an organization, and it can grow in its force and impact. But it won't just "happen." You can't beat something with nothing. And nature abhors a vacuum.

The default position—what fills the vacuum—is the *unthinking* organization.

Here's the problem: We can have really, really smart people and still not have a *Thinking Organization™*. We can pay a lot of money and spend a lot of energy to get these smart people, only to watch them use their smarts in non-constructive and petty and even destructive ways.

Let's say that 10 people are sitting in a room, wrestling with a new challenge or opportunity. Let's say further that they're all smart and have a reasonable level of commitment to the organization and to the topic at hand.

Let's call each of the 10 by their number.

- **Number 1** (the leader) is under pressure to come up with some answers or directions, and keeps the group on point by reminding them that there is no time to "fool around" or prolong the process.
- **Number 2** has been feeding Number 1 her pet ideas outside of the meeting and continually degrades the opinions of Numbers 3 through 10.
- **Number 3** is throwing out "You can't do it" and "This won't work" arguments faster than they can be addressed.
- **Number 4** wants to make sure that the policies and methods ensconced in current processes don't get tossed out or watered down.
- **Number 5** is afraid to sound stupid or be criticized and therefore appears to agree with whoever is speaking.
- **Number 6** keeps saying, in different ways, "Let's stick to our knitting; let's focus on what we know."
- **Number 7** reminds the group that the organization is the market leader and in the top quartile by all important measures, so any change should be approached very skeptically.
- **Number 8** goes back to one point over and over, as though nothing already said on that point has been mentioned or debated or decided.
- **Number 9** believes the group is at a clear fork in the road and that it has to choose one path or the other *now*.
- **Number 10** introduces the mystery of instinct, as he insists that everyone really knows "in their gut" which way the group should go.

Evaluate how often you see Numbers 1 through 10 (smart people acting collectively not-so-smart) in your organization.

In my organization,

I see the behavior of **Number 1:**
_____Almost all the time
_____Often
_____Sometimes
_____Almost never

I see the behavior of **Number 6:**
_____Almost all the time
_____Often
_____Sometimes
_____Almost never

I see the behavior of **Number 2:**
_____Almost all the time
_____Often
_____Sometimes
_____Almost never

I see the behavior of **Number 7:**
_____Almost all the time
_____Often
_____Sometimes
_____Almost never

I see the behavior of **Number 3:**
_____Almost all the time
_____Often
_____Sometimes
_____Almost never

I see the behavior of **Number 8:**
_____Almost all the time
_____Often
_____Sometimes
_____Almost never

I see the behavior of **Number 4:**
_____Almost all the time
_____Often
_____Sometimes
_____Almost never

I see the behavior of **Number 9:**
_____Almost all the time
_____Often
_____Sometimes
_____Almost never

I see the behavior of **Number 5:**
_____Almost all the time
_____Often
_____Sometimes
_____Almost never

I see the behavior of **Number 10:**
_____Almost all the time
_____Often
_____Sometimes
_____Almost never

Plan some action on this right now. And, by the way - are any of these *you*?

Meetings and discussions and projects sound like this sample meeting in most sectors of organizational life much of the time. Sometimes we find 2 "Number 3s" and 3 "Number 6s" (and no "Number 5s" or "Number 9s"), but the missing components don't measurably improve the thinking by their absence, and the reinforced components can take their specific deficiency to whole new levels of negativity and crippled thinking.

We can give up on all of this nonsense and start pitching overboard the people who disagree with us or most annoy us. But then we give up on the ability to think at all and settle for a comfortable, unthinking consensus—and we *still* have an unthinking organization.

What problems cause an organization to degenerate into an unthinking organization?

> **"A COMMITTEE IS A CUL-DE-SAC DOWN WHICH IDEAS ARE LURED AND THEN QUIETLY STRANGLED."**
>
> BARNETT COCKS,
> ATTRIBUTED[1]

Lowest-common-denominator negotiating – We have different ideas, but getting to an agreement is so...*hard*. So we keep going lower and lower, simpler and simpler, easier and easier, until we find a "solution" so harmless–and probably so worthless–that everyone can sign on.

Political compromise – We have a breakthrough idea, something with the real possibility of creating new value, but getting it through the reviews and approvals and power bases seems unlikely. So we start horse-trading and giving away the edges of the idea to get more support, and we give away more as it moves up the chain, until the idea still has enough pizzazz to get rejected as "dangerous" but not enough pizzazz to make a difference.

Lack of time to think – There's a lot of talk about the "knowledge economy" and "knowledge workers," but the fact is that getting the time to meditate and ruminate and doodle is a near impossibility in many organizations. We can experience the irony of being in a knowledge economy where our people never have time to think–or know *how* to think even if they do have time.

Questions that kill thought – Questions can easily be thought-exterminators. For example, we've seen first hand the continuously destructive power of the "either/or" question–"Should we do A or B?"—when the right answer is "Yes!"[2] For more on this topic, see the book *Broaden the Vision and Narrow the Focus: Managing in a World of Paradox*, where we explore 20 of the most prevalent paradoxes in business and organizational life.

Statements that kill thought – It's amazing how easily a single statement– especially from someone in authority–can stop thought cold. In our work with many organizations, we've uncovered the devastating power of statements like, "We've tried something like that before and it didn't work."[3]

The way we approach problems – The way we go about trying to solve a problem goes a long way toward determining the quality of our solutions. For example, saying "Let's look into X and Y, but let's not waste any time on Z" can end up annihilating us if Z is actually part or all of the answer.[4]

The use of dangerous words – There is a select group of words that are perfectly designed to annihilate thought. From "everyone" to "no one" and from "always" to "never," the absolute word is, in fact, most often the final word.

It isn't hard to be an unthinking organization. British statesman Edmund Burke observed, "All that is necessary for the triumph of evil is that good men do nothing."[5] In organizations, we could paraphrase this aphorism: "The only thing necessary for unthinking to triumph is for thinking people to do nothing."

"I HAVE A SAYING:
WE ARE ALL SMARTER TOMORROW."
GARY FROSSARD, PRESIDENT & CEO, KADEAN CONSTRUCTION CO.

ERADICATING 7 PROBLEMS THAT CAUSE UNTHINKING

On a scale of 1 to 10, rate your organization on each of the problems that causes unthinking in organizations. A rating of **1** means there is no evidence of this problem in your organization and **10** means your organization exemplifies this problem. In the space below each rating, write in an example of the problem that you have observed in your organization.

Lowest-common-denominator negotiating   1   2   3   4   5   6   7   8   9   10

_____

Political compromise   1   2   3   4   5   6   7   8   9   10

_____

Lack of time to think   1   2   3   4   5   6   7   8   9   10

_____

Questions that kill thought   1   2   3   4   5   6   7   8   9   10

_____

Statements that kill thought   1   2   3   4   5   6   7   8   9   10

_____

The way we approach problems   1   2   3   4   5   6   7   8   9   10

_____

The use of dangerous words   1   2   3   4   5   6   7   8   9   10

_____

"WHEN PEOPLE
APPLY THEMSELVES,
THEY CANNOT
HELP BUT LEARN.
FOR SOMEONE
WHO LACKS
APPLICATION,
EDUCATION
DOESN'T SEEM TO
HELP."

DAVID GREEN, CEO, HOBBY
LOBBY STORES

CLEAR-THINKING LEADERS AND ORGANIZATIONS

The Thinking Principle moves us toward clear thinking, toward basing our decisions and actions on crisp diagnosis and valid assessments. Clear thinking leaders and organizations take steps personally to ensure consistent and persistent clarity using the "10 Steps to Ensuring Clarity." They:

Step 1: Develop an unvarnished picture of external and internal truth to guide their decision making

Step 2: Base their organizational discussions around linear, reality-based thinking stripped of politics and fear

Step 3: Understand how to implant an organizational mindset that exploits change

Step 4: Foster widespread innovation at all levels in all areas on everything

Step 5: Intelligently assess and modify their strategies, structures and processes

Step 6: Encourage robust conflict and annihilate feeble consensus

Step 7: Exploit the communication glitches that typically cripple dialogue

Step 8: Manage the inevitable ignorance that pervades all organizations

Step 9: Convert the vast amounts of information—the deluge of information—into useful organizational knowledge and wisdom

Step 10: Ensure that what is thought about is shared with others as people create a *Teaching Organization*™

ASSESSING YOURSELF ON THE 10 STEPS TO ENSURING CLARITY

How would you rate yourself on these steps to ensuring clarity? A rating of **1** means that you are not currently intentional about taking this step, and **10** means that you consistently implement this step. In the space below each rating, write in an example of how you would like to improve on each of these.

Step 1. 1 2 3 4 5 6 7 8 9 10

I would like to improve:_____

Step 2. 1 2 3 4 5 6 7 8 9 10

I would like to improve:_____

Step 3. 1 2 3 4 5 6 7 8 9 10

I would like to improve:_____

Step 4. 1 2 3 4 5 6 7 8 9 10

I would like to improve:_____

Step 5. 1 2 3 4 5 6 7 8 9 10

I would like to improve:_____

Step 6. 1 2 3 4 5 6 7 8 9 10

I would like to improve:_____

Step 7. 1 2 3 4 5 6 7 8 9 10

I would like to improve:_____

Step 8. 1 2 3 4 5 6 7 8 9 10

I would like to improve:_____

Step 9. 1 2 3 4 5 6 7 8 9 10

I would like to improve:_____

Step 10. 1 2 3 4 5 6 7 8 9 10

I would like to improve:_____

DESIGNING
A *THINKING*
ORGANIZATION™

First, let's talk about design. Design means that we put the right things in the right place in the right order. We ask ourselves, "What is the right order? Where do we start to design an effective and powerfully *Thinking Organization*™?"

There are seven design factors–things we need to keep in mind as we put the Thinking Principle into practice.

Design Factor 1: Genetics

Design and build a thoughtful culture that embodies the *10 Key Elements of a Thinking Organization*™. We'll cover these individually later in the book, but here's the good news: You really can, methodically and in a growing way, incorporate these 10 cultural DNA points into your team or organization and actually make it think deeply.

Design Factor 2: Strategic Thinking

Develop deliberate, emerging, and evolving strategies in a *Strategic Planning Framework*™. Most strategies take whatever is being done and simply extrapolate those activities into the future, maybe with a few tweaks. Often, strategic planning is more about budgeting and setting up programs and projects than it is about evaluating how the organization will get from today to success. We need deliberate strategic thinking, where dedicated smart people focus on the possibilities. We need emerging strategic thinking, where all of our smart people have ways and means to input to the conversation. And we need evolving strategic thinking that melds the deliberate and emerging into a powerful channel into the future.

"I'VE SEEN THE FUTURE AND IT'S MUCH LIKE THE PRESENT, ONLY LONGER."

DAN QUISENBERRY, BASEBALL PITCHER[6]

Design Factor 3: Structural Optimization

Modify the structure to allow the team or organization to think smarter and more collaboratively. We need to eliminate the structural barriers to thinking across disciplines, functions, experience levels, and hierarchy.

Design Factor 4: Process Optimization

Ensure rational processes, quality systems, and relentlessly effective problem-solving methods. We want to have processes work for us, rather than having to work for the processes—an all-too-common scenario. We need to create and embed processes that help us–even cause us–to think better. And we need to modify or eliminate processes that prevent thought or foster stupid conversations.

Designing a Fearless Environment for Innovation

"You have to be in an environment where open-mindedness is encouraged," says Sheila Surgey, group marketing director at Hollard South Africa. "We want to coordinate and really release the energy of the organization."

After embarking on a significant reexamination of its vision and strategy, Hollard is now coordinating everyone around the newly articulated vision. For Surgey, this kind of alignment connects the organization's passion to its competencies: "Passion without purpose is of no use," she notes. "We get the best from people if they are passionate, but they have to be directed in the right direction with the right skills to be able to make the most of their passion."

In fact, says Surgey, the organization's ability to innovate and create value depends on whether people's passions align with the organization's larger vision.

"We find that a project that really has no passion behind it is almost doomed to failure at the beginning—when people are doing things because they are told to do them, not because they believe in what they are doing," Surgey observes. "If you are working on a project, why are you doing it? What is the big difference this project is going to make?"

Aligned around a vision for making a difference, Hollard focuses on sustaining a fearless culture where new ideas flourish and people find ways to make their passions into realities.

"Passion and open-mindedness to opportunity give you an ability to live out your own dreams—as long as they are aligned with the organization–and make a difference," says Surgey. "When you are more open-minded, natural innovative thinking comes into play. The word 'innovation' means 'relentless improvement' to us, and you can only relentlessly improve when you are open to learning."

Design Factor 5: Learning and Teaching

Really understand what moves the performance needle by converting company data and information into knowledge, truth, wisdom and competitive advantage. We have to take time to think and create forums where thinking is the main point on the agenda. And we need to get all that we know collectively on the table, moving far beyond the "learning organization" to become the *Teaching Organization*™.

Design Factor 6: Rational Management

Develop meaningful metrics, key performance indicators, critical success factors, and scorecards/dashboards on a foundation of *elegant simplicity*™. Few organizations really know how to manage what they know, in spite of efforts to improve "knowledge management." Unfortunately, knowledge management often degenerates into more technology–chat rooms, "knowledge networks," data warehouses–rather than taking what we know that is important, growing it, and converting it into *value*.

Design Factor 7: Intellectual Firepower™

Develop effective knowledge and accumulate a high level of *Thinking Capital*™. Organizations worry about financial and other sorts of capital but seldom worry about the one that drives innovation: the "thinking" variety of capital. This capital can be developed and grown and measured, but first we have to know that we need it.[7]

CRITICAL DESIGN QUESTIONS FOR THINKING ORGANIZATIONS

Consider what you think about thinking within your organization.

1. Right now, what is missing from our organization that is causing us not to think or to think poorly?

_____

_____

_____

2. In just a few sentences, what is our organization's approach to strategy?

_____

_____

_____

3. If we could change something about the current organizational structure to enhance the collective ability to think, what would it be?

_____

_____

_____

4. What attitudes or processes in the organization are the most crippling to effective thinking, and what could be done to minimize their influence (or even turn them to a support for thinking)?

_____

_____

_____

5. Name an opportunity or problem where a collective approach to learning, combined with a passionate commitment to teaching what we've learned, could make a big difference.

_____

_____

_____

6. What could we do right now to improve our management and the use of what we individually know?

_____

_____

_____

7. If "10" is "We make consistently brilliant decisions" and "1" is "We are drawn relentlessly toward stupid decisions," what is our organization's rating? _____
What is the first thing we should do to improve that rating?

_____

_____

_____

"PASSION IS CRITICAL IN INNOVATION. IT INSPIRES PEOPLE TO LOOK FOR EVEN MORE AND BETTER WAYS OF DOING THINGS, TO HEAR INPUT FROM OTHERS THAT WILL IMPROVE ON THE CURRENT IDEAS, AND TO OFFER IDEAS TO TEAM MEMBERS FOR IMPROVING PROCESSES AND PRODUCTS."

DAN AMSDEN, PRESIDENT, AUTOMATION ALLIANCE GROUP

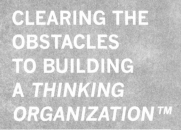

CLEARING THE OBSTACLES TO BUILDING A *THINKING ORGANIZATION*™

We've touched on some of the critical factors for designing a *Thinking Organization*™ or team. But to unlock the resources of the *Thinking Organization*™, we have to remove the obstacles that stand in our way. Let's take a look at some of the most common obstacles.

Obstacle 1: An Assumption that "Smart" = "Thinking"

Nobody wants to have a dumb organization. But in the absence of incentive, only a few will work hard to have a smart one. The easiest approach is to hire smart people and then hope that brilliance will take its natural course.

And of course, nature does take its course—*human* nature, that is. In the absence of a culture designed with the right cultural DNA, those smart people can actually work to the organization's detriment or even demise. The same "smarts" that can build can also destroy. Our finding: you are more likely to win with a team of reasonably intelligent people who know how to think together than you are with a group of extremely intelligent people who are in a culture designed to make them "stupid."

Obstacle 2: The Prevalence and Power of Ignorance

Peter Drucker once commented that the only thing in abundant supply in the universe is ignorance. Ignorance can be unwillful: we just don't know something, and we may not even know that we don't know it—or that it's even out there to be known. Or ignorance can be willful: the root of "ignorance" is the word "ignore," and smart people choose to ignore undeniable facts all the time.

Organizations often pretend that ignorance and incompetence can be avoided by good hiring and promotion practices. They suppose these problems can be eliminated through voluminous policies, procedures, and training. But these assumptions are delusional: ignorance, with its partner incompetence, is here to stay. In fact, everyone has some level of ignorance and incompetence in some aspect of life and perhaps even in some aspect of their own job. Ignorance and incompetence are not problems to be solved, but rather givens that need to be analyzed and thoughtfully improved where improvement is possible, or fenced in if they can't be improved.

> "IF YOU HAD TO IDENTIFY, IN ONE WORD, THE REASON WHY THE HUMAN RACE HAS NOT ACHIEVED, AND NEVER WILL ACHIEVE, ITS FULL POTENTIAL, THAT WORD WOULD BE 'MEETINGS.'"
>
> HUMORIST DAVE BARRY[8]

Obstacle 3: Structural or Process-Induced Turnover

Here's a fact of organizational life: morons are happy enough to work for a long time in a stifling, rigid, bureaucratic nightmare. But if you're a thinking person, you simply can't stand the mind-draining drivel that characterizes far too many organizations.

If every idea has to go up the "chain of command," if every decision needs 15 approvals where 3 would do the job, if following the rules is more important than creating value, then the really smart people are going to leave—unless of course we're paying them so much that they agree to commit mental suicide and stay.

Obstacle 4: Leaders Who Confuse "Activity" with "Performance"

It might seem obvious, but our experience says that activity isn't performance: You can't have a *Thinking Organization*™ without having or taking time to think.

I've had high-level people in very large organizations tell me, "Jim, we don't have time to make any significant changes. We can't take our eye off the ball. We have to stay with basic blocking and tackling. We can't afford any distractions. It's all about executing what we have in front of us." Their comments can be summarized as, "Thinking takes time, and we're too busy doing to think." There are too many things wrong with this approach to describe here, but suffice it to say that, in the mid- to long-term, there is no performance unless you think now—when you *don't* have the time.

"A MAN IS NOT IDLE BECAUSE HE IS ABSORBED IN THOUGHT. THERE IS A VISIBLE LABOR AND THERE IS AN INVISIBLE LABOR."

VICTOR HUGO, NOVELIST⁹

Obstacle 5: Desire for "Harmony"

Harmony, like motherhood and chocolate, is a hard thing to disparage. Who wouldn't want harmony? Who wouldn't want everyone to "get along"? Who wouldn't want everyone "pulling in the same direction"?

Well, I wouldn't. Totalitarian dictatorships have internal "harmony." The people driven to build the pyramids were all pulling in the same direction. Giving up the freedom to think and be and do in order to have harmony is a terrible trade. We'd better make sure that we don't have too much harmony.

Obstacle 6: Unthinking Authority

I've met many smart people who don't think. They think they're thinking, often because they're talking. But they stopped thinking a long time ago. Now they just recycle what they already "know" and say it with…well, authority.

If you're in authority, you have to force yourself to keep the thinking pathways open. It isn't easy, especially if you've made it to a point where you can think whatever you like and act on it. From time to time, when I see an organization struggling, I'll send the leadership a letter with one of my books, outlining some fresh ideas and inviting them to discuss the ideas pro bono. I don't really expect them to respond, and I'm usually not disappointed. But are they really so sure they've got all the answers?

If you're not in authority, and the one who is in charge isn't thinking, you have your work cut out for you. First, you have to keep thinking for yourself. Second, you have to keep feeding your ideas in, being careful to be creatively and graciously tenacious. Third, you have to produce some examples of places where fresh thinking improved results. And fourth, if all of this gets rebuffed, you have to go some place where thinking is considered a corporate asset.

Obstacle 7: The "One Best Way"

It's amazing how easily leaders and organizations can convince themselves that they have found the "one best way"–to reach customers, run a process, manage people, whatever. In the back of their minds, they know they can't have possibly found the one best way, but they push that thought away and simply act as though perfection has been discovered and implemented.

There is no one best way. Everything can be improved. Everything. Organizations, strategies, structures, processes, systems, policies, procedures, people, metrics–if it exists, it can be improved. But if it's the "one best way," it can't be improved–not because it's best but because it's unbending. Sooner or later, everyone will know that it's not the one best way, as times change or competitors smash us. The key is to know it sooner rather than later, and the only way to do that is to have a *Thinking Organization*™.

CLEARING THE OBSTACLES

On a scale of 1 to 10, rate your organization on each of the obstacles to building a *Thinking Organization*™. A rating of **1** means there is no evidence of this obstacle in your organization and **10** means your organization exemplifies this obstacle. In the space below each rating, for each rating above **3**, write in why you believe this obstacle exists in your organization and what might be done to clear the obstacle.

Obstacle 1: An assumption that "smart" = "thinking"

1 2 3 4 5 6 7 8 9 10

I believe this obstacle exists because:_____

To clear it we might:_____

Obstacle 2: The prevalence and power of ignorance

1 2 3 4 5 6 7 8 9 10

I believe this obstacle exists because:_____

To clear it we might:_____

Obstacle 3: Structural or process-induced turnover

1 2 3 4 5 6 7 8 9 10

I believe this obstacle exists because:_____

To clear it we might:_____

Obstacle 4: Leaders who confuse "activity" with "performance"

1 2 3 4 5 6 7 8 9 10

I believe this obstacle exists because:_____

To clear it we might:_____

Obstacle 5: Desire for "harmony"

1 2 3 4 5 6 7 8 9 10

I believe this obstacle exists because:_____

To clear it we might:_____

Obstacle 6: Unthinking authority

1 2 3 4 5 6 7 8 9 10

I believe this obstacle exists because:_____

To clear it we might:_____

Obstacle 7: The "one best way"

1 2 3 4 5 6 7 8 9 10

I believe this obstacle exists because:_____

To clear it we might:_____

"MEN FEAR THOUGHT AS THEY FEAR NOTHING ELSE ON EARTH, MORE THAN RUIN, MORE EVEN THAN DEATH. THOUGHT IS SUBVERSIVE AND REVOLUTIONARY, DESTRUCTIVE AND TERRIBLE, THOUGHT IS MERCILESS TO PRIVILEGE, ESTABLISHED INSTITUTIONS, AND COMFORTABLE HABIT."

BERTRAND RUSSELL, MATHEMATICIAN[10]

BUILDING A *THINKING* *ORGANIZATION*™

Now that we're beginning to put our design in place and clear out the obstacles, we can think about building. Because every industry, every organization, and every group of people will be different, each building process will be unique.

There are, however, 10 Keys to keep in mind as we build our *Thinking Organization*™. These 10 Keys grow out of Luman's more than 25 years of work helping our clients build *Thinking Organizations*™. Here they are:

Key 1: Positive Discontent

We're not happy–and we're really happy about that. Being passionate doesn't mean being "positive," at least in the usual sense of "happy." We can be positive and still be unhappy – unhappy with restrictive structures and burdensome processes and stupid rules. This is what we mean by *positive discontent*™ – we have an eye out for anything that keeps us from living passionate, successful lives together, and then we're constructive in how we suggest alternatives or recommend solutions.

There are dozens of "Management 101" courses out there to teach us how to manage and eliminate conflict. What we want to do is find numerous ways to encourage and amplify *productive* conflict. We want to implement the radical idea of "managing consensus so it doesn't get out of hand." The difference is huge between consensus *before* all thoughts are explored and consensus *after* all thoughts are explored, and it makes all the difference.

Key 2: Abandonment

We give up the old to seize the new. Nothing changes unless something old disappears. You can't build a new building on a site until the old, dilapidated one is torn down. *Thinking Organizations*™ are superb at abandonment–not only letting go of the past, but tossing it overboard with satisfaction and confidence. Of course, there must be much analysis and discussion before a strategy or product or service is abandoned. But when it's clear that whatever we're talking about isn't working well (or at all), Abandonment DNA says "Enough! Let's move forward!"

Much has been written about "critical thinking," and much of that writing is about mechanisms, tools, and templates to allow an individual or team to think accurately about a given problem or situation. There's some value there. But

> "THE WORLD WE HAVE CREATED IS A PRODUCT OF OUR THINKING; IT CANNOT BE CHANGED WITHOUT CHANGING OUR THINKING."
>
> ALBERT EINSTEIN, PHYSICIST[11]

really critical thinking is a skill needed by every person, every day, at every level. It involves a critical evaluation on an ongoing basis of the value of any given activity, decision, or process. Change is often viewed as an event or an initiative or a process, and less often as what it really is: a *mindset*. But a *Thinking Organization*™ is rooted in the exploitation of change–rapidly abandoning the outmoded and useless to embrace the new and daring–and becoming a way of life rather than an event *or* a process.

Key 3: Boldness

We choose to go until we have to stop. Too many leaders are too tentative and force their organizations or teams to hesitate, procrastinate, deliberate, and pontificate (about all the reasons that daring thought and action should be postponed). They have to have a reason–or many reasons, or impossible-to-ignore reasons–before they will think about fresh ideas or audacious directions. "Better safe than sorry" is their mantra.

They forget that we can be safe and *still* be sorry. In fact, we can be even sorrier because we were playing it so safe. Where were the brave people to ask,

- "Are people really going to keep buying trucks and SUVs as gasoline prices rise with global industrialization?"
- "Doesn't this 'hub' system have the possibility of making our airline incredibly inefficient?"
- "Can we really outsource all of our customer service to people 5,000 miles away?"
- "Will we be able to run the world's economy effectively on burning dinosaur remains?"
- "Are you sure stocks/housing/oil/commodities will keep going up indefinitely?"

Thinking leaders recruit new ideas before reality forces them to change.

"I had always had this idea of putting a story on t-shirts," says Tammy Hotsenpiller, co-founder and designer of the Humanity™ for All clothing line. "My vision was to take a t-shirt and write a story on the inside and then explain the story graphically on the outside."

From this one very original idea has sprung a company that often looks more like a movement than a simple business concern.

The story began when Hotsenpiller explained her concept to a colleague she had met through an executive coaching partnership. "One thing led to another," Hotsenpiller recalls, "and I visited her at her factory, which is the largest manufacturer of couture t-shirts in the United States, with over 700 employees in the Los Angeles area. She was very modest and humble. We sat down, and she asked what it was going to look like."

Soon, Hotsenpiller was pulling together a team of friends and colleagues and designing the first shirt. "The first story I wrote was about Mother Teresa. On the train on the way to Calcutta, she received a calling to help the poorest of the poor," Hotsenpiller says. That story was printed inside the shirt, along with words from Mother Teresa's Nobel Prize acceptance speech. Hotsenpiller began collaborating with an artist, who drew the story for the back of the shirt.

As the team grew, the ideas multiplied. The stories the shirts tell now fall into three categories: individuals, social justice, and the environment. One line of shirts exemplifies the 30 Articles of the United Nations' Universal Declaration of Human Rights. A shirt printed with a story about going green was worn by the presenter at Film Independent's Spirit Awards.

"People can wear their passions," says Hotsenpiller. "They can tell their stories of life and show their passions on their t-shirts." While the edgy art displays the wearer's passions to the world, the story inside the shirt is a deeply personal reminder of the people and ideas that inspire those passions.

The concept soon proved too potent to contain, as Hotsenpiller explains. "We realized that we have a movement here, not a clothing line. People started approaching us from all walks of life: the Red Cross, the Halle Berry Foundation, and numerous other non-profit organizations—Redefine Reality, which works with people with eating disorders, and Mercy Ministries, which has homes for girls with emotional issues. We started co-branding with organizations, telling their stories."

Soon, corporations and celebrities who wanted to promote the Humanity™ themes were also joining the movement. The line has found its way into boutique shops across the

United States. It's sported by movie stars. Major entertainment corporations have asked Humanity™ to develop lines for them.

"Humanity™ is bringing people, ideas, companies, and passions together to make a difference," says Hotsenpiller. "We believe we're doing something that has never been done before. We are branding a concept, a movement. It's a conviction. We are inviting people to join the Humanity™ network. If we say that Humanity™ is for everyone, we have to have something other than a product. We have to have opportunity."

The secret to fueling innovation and adding financial and social value, Hotsenpiller argues, is keeping herself focused and the company centered on its values.

"To bring diverse groups and people together to work towards a common goal, I first had to know who I am in my core," she says. "I had to know what I could contribute. Then I had to know what I was looking for. It's really easy to get sidetracked with someone else's passion, someone else's view. You can't compromise. You have to establish the core of the company and where you want to go, yet you have to have open hands to determine whether or not you want to move in a new direction."

For Hotsenpiller, the rewards of leading an inventive company far outweigh the costs. "I've poured a lot of finances and energy into this, without seeing the reward yet other than just the opportunities," she says. "My husband asked me, 'Would you do this if you knew you were never going to be paid for it?' and I said, 'Absolutely.'" But Hotsenpiller seems unlikely to stop there.

"Everything is possible," she affirms, "if you have a clear message, if you have a plan, and if you take it step by step."

Key 4: Curiosity

There are some interesting things we don't yet know. Curiosity is defined as "an eager desire to know; inquisitive."[12] Curiosity isn't wanting to know new stuff; it's *really* wanting to know new stuff. If we're curious, we know that at all times there is something interesting and important out there that we don't yet know. We have an exploratory mindset. We ask a lot of questions–to learn rather than to show off. We'd rather take the criticism, "Can't you just stop trying new things and focus?" than "You mean you really haven't thought about that possibility?"

When most people hear the terms "innovation" or "creativity," their typical response is, "Oh, you mean research and development? Or product development?" But in the *Thinking Organization™*, innovation and creativity are expected from every person in every area, every day. No matter how humdrum our product or service, curiosity can drive us toward creating a wildly innovative culture. But we'll have to push ourselves because the draw of the familiar and comfortable is very strong.

Key 5: Humility

We never overestimate ourselves or underestimate others. When we're passionate about something, we face the danger of moving from confidence to cockiness, and then it's a short trip to arrogance. We need to remember–we need to *force* ourselves to remember–how much we don't know. We have to seek out anyone who can teach us what we don't know. We want to push ourselves to be open to–and prize– anyone who points out the fallacies of what we *think* we know. And we're secure enough to give credit to all who contribute to the development of an idea.

We resist making the easy assumption that others don't know anything that could be useful to us. Children, young people, new employees, fresh graduates, uneducated workers, taxi drivers, wait staff–no one is here by accident; everyone has something locked away–even if it's only a bad example–that can teach us and make us just a little bit smarter.

Key 6: Listening

We allow others to change us by what they say. Listening–really listening–is, for some reason, a very hard thing to do. We've all been in those conversations where we can tell this or that person isn't listening at all but is merely waiting for someone to catch his breath so he can jump in with his flashing light of brilliance. But listening is a prerequisite for thinking, the exercise that gets us out of our own re-circulating thoughts and too-early conclusions and makes us consider and reconsider. Real listening is a collaborative enterprise, in which we allow other people to impact our thinking by what they say.

It's been said that "We only learn when we listen, and not when we talk," but this isn't true. We can indeed learn when we talk, if we're still forming our thoughts and using their public display as a way to develop and shape them. But it's certainly true that we have a much more consistent opportunity to learn when we're listening than when we're talking.

Key 7: Reflection

The unexamined organization isn't worth living in. Organizational life is played out in its strategies, structures, and processes. These are typically viewed as fixed or solid, but in reality, they are constantly in flux whether we admit it or not. In the unthinking organization, they are

"THOUGHT BREEDS THOUGHT. IT GROWS UNDER YOUR HANDS."

HENRY DAVID THOREAU, PHILOSOPHER[13]

allowed to deteriorate until a full-scale correction—perhaps even triage—is required. In the *Thinking Organization™*, these are evaluated and corrected incrementally so that higher levels of performance are achieved and the "big adjustments" can be avoided. We examine ourselves and our objectives on a regular basis and remember that much of what distinguishes success from failure can be summed up in one phrase: relentless realism.

Reflection requires us to carve out time to think about what we "know" and don't know. We don't accept problems and arguments the way they are presented to us, but try to dig down deep to find out what's really going on. At the same time, we don't discount ideas or input because of the person who is speaking or the way they are saying it. It's a reason to pause and reconsider; it doesn't matter that it's coming from an idiot or a brute. We take the time to decide how to decide, and we're always willing to dig deeper on things that have already been decided. And we remember that problem solving is all about thinking, and that all too many problems are addressed with heavy emphasis on producing quick solutions and little emphasis on the thinking that can make those solutions powerful.

Key 8: Complementarity

We believe that clarity arises from seeing the whole picture. One of the greatest disasters in leadership thinking is the false "either/or"—creating a choice, tradeoff, or conflict where one only exists in our thinking and not in reality.

- "Do we want a passionate work force or a focus on results?"
- "Should we concentrate on the present or the future?"
- "Should we exercise authority or share power?"
- "Do we need to take more risks or eliminate risk?"
- "Should we move faster or take more time?"

The answer to these "either/or" questions is, "Yes!" We want both, we want it all. We know that only whole solutions, solutions that incorporate both ideas, can lead to clear thinking and world-class decisions. We know that we can optimize and exploit the group's collective intelligence. And we never answer a "both/and" question with an "either/or" answer.

This Key is so important to living a passionate and successful life that we have devoted a separate book to helping you master and benefit from this powerful principle: *The Paradox Principle: How Passionate Leaders Merge Competing Ideas*, the fourth title in the PASSIONATE LIVES & LEADERS series. In it we look at *personal* paradoxes that will affect your leadership and career, for good or for bad depending on how you address them. (If you're a leader, you might want a rich and accessible treatment of *organizational* paradoxes. This can be found in the book *Broaden the Vision and Narrow the Focus: Managing in a World of Paradox.)*[14]

> "A GREAT TRUTH IS A TRUTH WHOSE OPPOSITE IS ALSO TRUE."
>
> THOMAS MANN, GERMAN NOVELIST AND NOBEL LAUREATE[15]

Key 9: Range

We expect diversity of thought and lots of it. We can have a lot of smart people working on an issue and still come up with stupid ideas if we're missing range. If we all have the same background, training, or chosen perspective, it's unlikely–maybe even impossible–that we will do the famous "thinking outside the box." The box is too small, and the lid is on too tight.

When we want range, we *insist* on a multidisciplinary viewpoint. We want to hear from anyone who could possibly have a "take" on the question or topic at hand, and possibly from others who have no direct knowledge about it at all. It's amazing, for example, what history, biology, and music theory can teach us about business. With range, we *require* diversity of thought. We want 10 ideas or 10 people–or both–and not the "one best way" or the "expert" alone. We reward rather than punish fresh thinking, and we refuse to discriminate against anyone because of the color of their thinking.

"I've been around a lot of amazing people," says actor Emily Rose, "and I've learned a lot of amazing things purely because I've had an attitude to discover how the best people go about their work and how they write their material and deal with stressful auditions."

Rose's openness to learning from a diverse array of artists has helped her to take the guesswork out of the creative process and the acting profession. Her approach has clearly paid off: she has had recurring roles in hit television shows like Brothers and Sisters *and* ER, *and she has guest starred on others, like* Cold Case *and* Without a Trace. *In fact, she has recently landed the lead in a new show.*

But while she surrounds herself with people who can show her the ropes, Rose has also taken risks and embraced the solitary side of her art. She argues that innovators and creators cannot wait for someone else to hire them or create work for them.

"Whatever you have a passion to do, start doing it, even on your own," she advises. "If you want to do something, start creating on your own. Take a stab at things."

From her mentors and colleagues, Rose has acquired artistic rigor that she might have struggled for years to attain without their input. But she often achieves that precision and craft through a process that looks anything but neat.

"When I would go out for a partnered audition, I used to get so frustrated at myself for procrastinating or having to put the material down for a little period of time, but I learned that that's part of my creative process," she says. It's an insight she recommends to others.

"As a creative person," she explains, "give yourself grace to be messy when you're creating. We go to school in a linear, black-and-white way of learning. I never learned well that way. I had to be a hands-on, messy, finger-painting kind of a girl. You have to be okay with your own creative process and the way that you work."

Key 10: Precision

We can think messy, but we can't think sloppy. Being precise isn't the same as being perfect. In fact, mistakes can be a great aid in becoming more precise, if we treat them properly. Many leaders have some vague sense that failure and mistakes are not all bad. But mistakes seem so contradictory to high performance that they're usually chastised, abused, and made to cower in the corner rather than allowed to provide any real value to the organization. Organizations often fail to systematize the process for gleaning value from every failure and mistake.

If we are passionately precise, we hate "sloppy thinking." We avoid broad generalizations and loose approximations. We strive for accuracy in thought as a prelude to word, decision, and action. We use illustrations and anecdotes appropriately, as *illustrations* of a position and not as *proof* of a position.

At the same time, we're open to well-thought-out, nuanced generalizations and intelligent approximations. And we thoughtfully convert data into useful information, information into useful knowledge (what we *know* to be true), knowledge into useful truth (the knowledge that we have defined and refined by practicing), and truth into organization-wide wisdom (the truth that we have firmly embedded into our organizational character and actions).

"READ, EVERY DAY, SOMETHING NO ONE ELSE IS READING. THINK, EVERYDAY, SOMETHING NO ONE ELSE IS THINKING. DO, EVERY DAY, SOMETHING NO ONE ELSE WOULD BE SILLY ENOUGH TO DO. IT IS BAD FOR THE MIND TO CONTINUALLY BE PART OF UNANIMITY."

CHRISTOPHER MORLEY, JOURNALIST[16]

On a scale of 1 to 10, rate your organization on each of the keys. A rating of **1** means there is no evidence of this key in your organization, and **10** means your organization exemplifies the key trait.

Positive Discontent	1	2	3	4	5	6	7	8	9	10
Abandonment	1	2	3	4	5	6	7	8	9	10
Boldness	1	2	3	4	5	6	7	8	9	10
Curiosity	1	2	3	4	5	6	7	8	9	10
Humility	1	2	3	4	5	6	7	8	9	10
Listening	1	2	3	4	5	6	7	8	9	10
Reflection	1	2	3	4	5	6	7	8	9	10
Complementarity	1	2	3	4	5	6	7	8	9	10
Range	1	2	3	4	5	6	7	8	9	10
Precision	1	2	3	4	5	6	7	8	9	10

"GENIUS IS THE CAPACITY FOR TAKING INFINITE PAINS."

THOMAS CARLYLE[17]

Now, jot down why you assigned each score and what could be done to improve it.

Positive Discontent _____

_____

Abandonment _____

_____

Boldness _____

_____

Curiosity _____

_____

Humility _____

_____

Listening _____

_____

Reflection _____

_____

Complementarity _____

_____

Range _____

_____

Precision _____

_____

Take your two or three lowest scores and meet with your team to brainstorm ways to improve them. Get an outside facilitator to help if necessary. The goal is to build a *Thinking Organization*™ by design, from the inside out, so sustainable success will be yours.

GETTING
INNOVATION
EVERYWHERE

While I was in Morocco facilitating a global conference for leaders from a multinational company, I watched as an understandable–but extremely narrow– scene unfolded.

This high-tech company had just selected 8 core values that would guide it in the new millennium. We broke the attendees (about 100 people) into 8 groups to discuss what those values would "look like" in practice– what mindset these values should produce, what behaviors they should encourage and discourage, and how they could be applied in the everyday life of the company.

People from all parts of the organization were blended on all of the "values discussion" teams, except one: the innovation team. The only people who thought they should be on this team (in fact, the only people whom everyone in the company thought should be on this team) were scientists and engineers who had the specific function of doing research. As so often happens, innovation got put in a box.

Often, when we think about "innovation," we think of "research and development" or "new products and services." This is a good place to start, and these areas certainly represent critical focus points for innovation. But when we limit innovation to these functions, we miss the vast potential that our organizations hold for creating value.

"WHEN PEOPLE WITH PASSION COLLABORATE, INEVITABLY THEY THINK OUT OF THE PROVERBIAL BOX. PASSIONATE AND ENGAGED EMPLOYEES DARE TO DREAM AND ENVISION THE 'WHAT IF' SCENARIOS. THEY CAN IMAGINE THE ULTIMATE RESULT AND FIGURE OUT A WAY TO ACHIEVE IT."

DEBORAH MCINTYRE, VICE PRESIDENT WELLS FARGO BANK

What would happen if everyone–and I mean everyone–were committed to innovating in his or her current assignments? What if the norm becomes creating and evolving and changing rather than maintaining and extrapolating and resisting? What kind of opportunity is just waiting out there to be tapped by the wise, shrewd, passionate leader?

In most organizations, there are thousands of untapped ideas that could add value (help us play the current game better) or create value (help us play a different game). There is a reservoir, an underground aquifer, of ideas and suggestions and possibilities that most formal leaders never even recognize, much less access.

ADDING AND CREATING VALUE

Take a few minutes—or a lunch—to think about your work and your team in a fresh way. Now jot down 3 to 5 ideas on what could be done better (adding value) or differently (creating value):

We could do these things *better*:

1. _____

2. _____

3. _____

4. _____

5. _____

Other possibilities for doing things better (if any): _____

_____

_____

We could do these things *differently*:

1. _____

2. _____

3. _____

4. _____

5. _____

Other possibilities for doing things differently (if any):

_____

_____

_____

_____

To be sure, some of these ideas may only be fragments. But each one has potential to make work and life better.

Now take a few more minutes–or another lunch–to outline a brief "game plan" for taking action on one item from each of the above possibility lists:

Game plan for doing Item Number _____ better:

_____

_____

_____

_____

_____

Game plan for doing Item Number _____ differently:

_____

_____

_____

_____

_____

A few organizations have found a way to get an average of 10, 20, or even more than 50 ideas from every employee *every year.* Most of us would fall off our chairs if we got 2 or 3. And what's the story in the vast majority of organizations Luman International has researched? Less than 1 per person.

Look at the potential consequences. If there are two organizations of 100 people in the same industry, and one gets 0.5 ideas per employee and the other gets 50 per employee, how different will their results be? 50 ideas versus 5,000?

It's no contest.

Even when people have a potentially valuable insight, they're unlikely to develop it if there's no "payoff." And by "payoff," we don't necessarily (or even primarily) mean money or other physical rewards (although those are nice ideas). We mean things like:

- Acknowledging their ideas
- Thanking them for their ideas
- Welcoming input
- Finding inexpensive ways of recognizing creativity
- Giving people time or resources to explore their ideas

Perhaps some of the "half-baked" ideas floating around our organizations are half-baked only because we're not providing any ovens.

So how do we really get innovation everywhere? Well, we aren't going to get it by putting suggestion boxes in the office or plant or by telling people that we're "open" to their input.

I remember asking one leader how he got input from his people. He said he used a suggestion box. When I asked him how many ideas he had gotten in the last month,

> "FEW PEOPLE THINK MORE THAN TWO OR THREE TIMES A YEAR. I HAVE MADE AN INTERNATIONAL REPUTATION FOR MYSELF BY THINKING ONCE OR TWICE A WEEK."
>
> GEORGE BERNARD SHAW, PLAYWRIGHT[18]

he sheepishly replied that he hadn't checked the box that month (now there's a vibrant system!). He had to get his keys to unlock the box. (Amused, I asked him if he was afraid that one of his people might break into the box and use the ideas). He unlocked the box, which was—to my surprise—full.

Of *candy* wrappers. What does *that* say to an organization's leadership?

If we're going to get widespread innovation, we're going to have to use both more and different approaches. We're going to have to do the hard work of organizational rethinking and redesign. We're going to need to turn the keys of innovation to unlock the doors to widespread creativity.

Door 1: Belief That Widespread Innovation Is Possible

We have to believe (in spite of the reality that some people just don't care) that most people would like to feel good about what they're doing and would like to make a contribution to doing it better.

We have to trust that the urge to create is inherent in human beings, a quality that schools and organizations and life tend to disregard or crush. And we have to accept that something powerful can happen when ideas begin to flow and collide and intermingle with others.

Door 2: Measurement, Recognition, and Reward of Innovation

We have to find ways to measure—yes, measure—recognize, and reward innovation, from the small $500 procedure improvement to the $50,000 process enhancement. Any cutting-edge leader senses today that constant innovation is critical if the organization is to survive, much less thrive. And yet, few leaders have taken the (arguably challenging) approach of measuring innovation.

If what gets measured gets done, and what gets rewarded gets done well, then we have to find ways to apply this truth to innovation.

One idea we have used successfully is to have everyone maintain an "Innovation Log." Everyone uses the same form, which looks something like this:

INNOVATION LOG

Date _____

Description of Idea _____

_____

_____

Expected Impact (savings, increased revenues, customer service improvements,

etc.) _____

_____

_____

Expected Costs (resources needed to implement, learning curve costs, process

change costs, etc.) _____

_____

_____

Was the idea implemented? (circle one)   Y   N   If not, why?

_____

_____

_____

Was the idea implemented without approval? (circle one)   Y   N   Why?

_____

_____

_____

Who was affected by the idea?

_____

_____

_____

Who helped to develop the idea?

_____

_____

_____

We tell people, "You can turn in a blank page at the end of the year, but, of course, the part of your future that relates to creativity and innovation will also be blank." If you take the next step and post these logs, you not only recognize people for their ideas and prompt others to do the same, but you also provide a lot of food for thought and will spur innovation in other areas.

Door 3: An Environment Where Creativity Can Flourish

The only way that leaders can get innovation everywhere is to become organizational designers–to create an environment where creativity can flourish. This task isn't a matter of building a "system" of innovation. Formulas tend to squelch rather than encourage people to open up their minds and mouths.

It is a matter of creating a safe place for dangerous change.

There are crucial factors that create an environment where innovation becomes a perpetual motion machine. Here are 5 things that great leaders should find themselves doing in their supreme role of organizational designer:

- **Focusing on possibilities rather than limitations**. Most organizations are focused on limitations. This focus can take the form of written restrictions (like policy and procedure manuals) or unwritten restrictions (such as, "This isn't the way we do things around here"). It's too easy to design our organizations to take care of the 5 to 10 percent of people who will take advantage of us rather than the 90 to 95 percent who will create value for us if we provide the setting. The result? The 5 percent still take advantage of us, and the 95 percent are shackled and silent.

  We need to ask ourselves, "How can we focus on freedom and opportunity rather than control and negativity?" We have to acknowledge that we can't get positive energy out of a negative culture. Every year, we need to ask every employee, "How will we be different in 3 years *because of you?*" If we want to make it to the playoffs, we want impact players at every position.

- **Building a *powersharing*™ culture.** Over the past 20 years, hierarchical structures have given way to "empowerment" on paper, if not in the minds of many leaders. But what does "empowerment" really say? "I'm the leader and you're not, but I'm such a gracious leader, I'm going to bestow a little of my 'power' on you." All too often in practice, this means the responsibility and accountability get passed down but not the commensurate authority and resources to get the job done creatively.

  "Empowerment" must be replaced by a true *powersharing*™ culture if we want high-order innovation everywhere. This means that we have to search out and eliminate what is causing our people to stay on the sidelines and play it safe. We have to ask ourselves, "How do we get everyone into the game? How do we get everyone to invest themselves in this place?" One of the differentiating factors between average and high-performing organizations is the originating point of new ideas. In average organizations, the vast majority of the ideas come from the top. In high-performing organizations, the vast majority of ideas come from below. Is that really a surprise? Who knows the work better than the people who are doing it?[19]

- **Becoming a maverick-friendly environment.** In far too many organizations, the only place where somebody can be a maverick is at the top. Mavericks elsewhere are boxed in, ostracized, criticized, and fired. We can think we're doing well as leaders when we simply "tolerate" them. But as long as mavericks are viewed in our organizations as poor team players, disloyal, or simply strange, we're unlikely to get much of anything except *groupthink*.

Leaders who produce innovative cultures find ways to nurture, encourage, celebrate, and promote these people. They know that creativity only comes from people who are allowed and encouraged to think creatively. And by the way, who *are* these people? Practically everyone who works for us, if we will create a risk-friendly and mistake-friendly home for them. We have to ask ourselves, "How can we create a safe place for 'dangerous' people?"

- **Centralizing by shared vision and values rather than structure.** Every leader, sooner or later, faces this critical question: "Should we centralize, or should we decentralize?" From the biggest operations like General Electric or Toyota to the smallest, organizations have wrestled with this question and alternated between the two options. But the answer is "yes." We need to do both. We have to have both unity and diversity, both a common focus and a variable way of focusing.

In a sense, this is even the wrong question. The real question is, "Should we centralize by a shared sense of purpose and values, or should we centralize by a rigid, funneling structure?" We can't do both, and most organizations have opted for the latter. The great ones – the great leaders – opt for centralizing by shared vision and values and mutual trust, which is a lot harder to do than drafting organization charts and writing rules. The reason they do this is that it actually *works*. Great leaders know this is the only way to produce high performance and invested employees. So we have to ask ourselves, "How can we centralize around mutuality of purpose and character rather than hierarchy and fear?"

- **Marking all ideas "Fragile: Handle with Care."** What do we do with ideas when someone actually has the courage to present them? Do we react strongly or negatively? Do we immediately focus on all the reasons that the ideas can't possibly work? Do we criticize these ideas from all sides before we even understand them or their potential influence? Do we simply frown and say, "I'll have to think about that" – while saying all the time with our tone and body language, "*That'll* never happen!"

We have to recognize that new ideas are like infants: they have to be treated with care because they're so small and helpless. We have to put some of them in "incubators" – with a champion, a department, a team that can protect them and get them through those rough early days. We can't hold them up to the same standards of financial return or payback as we can with a mature product or service or process. We have to ask ourselves, "How do we nurture new ideas and prevent them from getting annihilated by routine, the status quo, and extrapolation of old ways into the future?"

Leaders who don't do these things are not really leaders at all. They are presiding over an enterprise that is, at best, far less than excellent and, at worst, a journey to oblivion.

But leaders who take these steps in organizational design will watch innovation grow – everywhere.

DESIGNING AN ENVIRONMENT WHERE CREATIVITY CAN FLOURISH

Think about your organization, and jot down at least one change you would make in response to each of these critical questions.

1. How can we focus on freedom and opportunity rather than control and negativity?

_____

_____

_____

2. How do we get everyone into the game? How do we get everyone to invest themselves in this place?

_____

_____

_____

3. How can we create a safe place for 'dangerous' people?

_____

_____

_____

4. How can we centralize around mutuality of purpose and character rather than hierarchy and fear?

_____

_____

_____

5. How do we nurture new ideas and prevent them from getting annihilated by routine and the status quo and extrapolation of old ways into the future?

_____

_____

_____

We can try to open up innovation by providing technology – intranets, corporate yellow pages, access to "SMEs" (Subject Matter Experts), knowledge networks, social networks – all of which are good ideas. But none of this will work if the culture is closed. Technology and tools will never override or overcome a defective culture. If we think otherwise, we are operating under a truly fatal illusion.

We've all heard that knowledge is power. But for most people, it's power when it is *hoarded* rather than when it is *shared*. As a result, tacit knowledge is filling the culture, but there's no way to access it, to see it combined with other knowledge in ways that will grow something new.

You can change that sad fact by designing a place where pervasive innovation can live and grow.

All of our people have it in their power to do nothing. We can make people come to work (sort of) and discharge their responsibilities (sort of), but we can't make them be creative. We can't force innovation or trick people into producing a new idea.

But we can do something. We can open the doors and windows and let the fresh air of freedom and opportunity revive all of that long-buried creativity.

Finding the Music

Ran Jackson was singing opera and taking classical lessons in college, but he kept thinking about something else, a question that ran through his head like a song: "How can I use this for rock and roll?"

When Jackson left high school, he and his brother had formed a band, and it was during college that they started writing music more seriously—rock music, "to our professors' dismay," he remembers.

But the fusion of classical training and a rock sensibility gave them a unique resource for musical innovation. Their demos somehow made it into the hands of producers in Nashville, and after being flown out to Nashville a number of times, the brothers ended up signing with Warner Brothers. Still in college, they went full-time into music, moving to Nashville and starting The Daylights.

The eclectic influences on which Jackson draws don't just come from music. "I think there are a lot of things I still want to do outside of music," he says. "I think those are all things that will happen in their time, and they're all things that infiltrate into what I'm doing at a different level."

Still, Jackson insists that creative work requires focusing his diverse resources on an area of strength. "I know I wouldn't make a great politician or scientist," he admits, "but I think I have the best potential to be a great musician. If I didn't think I did, I definitely would do something else. A lot of people can do a lot of things really well, but find that one thing that is done inherently well, the gift that God has given you."

For Jackson, that gift occupies a powerful place in his life.

"Music has been a foundational bone in my body," he says. "It was almost outside of my choosing. I'm in it because I love telling stories with music and song and seeing what it does to the listener. I love it and feed off of it. It's definitely part of who I am."

"SOME PEOPLE MISTAKE WEAKNESS FOR TACT. IF THEY ARE SILENT WHEN THEY OUGHT TO SPEAK AND SO FEIGN AN AGREEMENT THEY DO NOT FEEL, THEY CALL IT BEING TACTFUL. COWARDICE WOULD BE A MUCH BETTER NAME."

FRANK MEDLICOTT[20]

MANAGING CONSENSUS SO IT DOESN'T GET OUT OF HAND

Here is *Luman's Law of Consensus*: *Great leaders manage consensus so it doesn't get out of hand.*

The Problem with Consensus

We've all seen the courses offered by the seminar companies with the theme, "How to manage conflict so it doesn't get out of hand."

Conflict can indeed be disastrous. Personality clashes, turf battles, runaway ambitions, differing viewpoints, authority issues, unbreakable deadlines, stress, carelessness, stupid mistakes – the causes of conflict are endless. In some organizations, they all seem to be operating with full force at the same time. It's why the seminar companies are able to use "managing conflict" as a money-making staple.

But bad conflict can be so bad that it can blind us to the value of good conflict. We can miss the robustness of conclusions that flow from healthy debate. There are some things worth fighting about. Organizational vision, mission, values, strategy, value proposition, offerings, brand, identity – the things that make us who we are and determine our direction should never be decided without a lot of conflict.

But bad conflict can also blind us to the destructiveness of bad consensus. We can miss the robustness of conclusions that flow from a well-considered refusal to agree.

What we need is healthy, open conflict about critical issues and hard-to-achieve, deep-rooted consensus about important decisions. What we often get is the default position: unhealthy, back-room conflict on petty issues and easy-to-achieve, fake consensus on important decisions.

Luman's Law of Consensus reminds us that we should be a little less focused on harmony and a lot more focused on managing consensus so we aren't wiped out by agreement.

What is bad consensus? It's phony agreement. It's agreement that isn't real, or if it's real, it isn't deep. It's the "course of least resistance," and it ends up in one of two ways:

1. The lowest-common-denominator, the "best" decision that everyone will "support" without creating World War III (which usually means a decision or direction with no effective firepower); or

2. Going along with the boss because it's by and large easier to feign agreement with powerful people than to express difference with them (which usually means a decision or direction with no effective support).

The first is often more about what's left out than what's done, and it's why teams are often so poor at adding or creating real value. The second can end up with better results than the first, *as long as the boss is right*. If he or she is wrong, the results can be worse than the lowest common denominator – and the stronger the personality, the greater the chance of disaster and the lower the chance of anyone speaking up until it's too late.

At Luman International, we worked with one large organization that had been very top-down in its selection process for projects for investment. One of the biggest projects they had ever attempted seemed to have support up and down the line, until everything went to perdition and the company faced a loss of hundreds of millions of dollars.

Then the voices of dissent came out of hiding, long after they could do any good. *Then* almost everyone knew that the project was a bad idea. *Then* many of them had proof that they had *always* felt that way. *Then* people were fired and demoted and transferred. But the honest truth was that the problem was systemic. The organization was perfectly designed to get consensus, whatever the cost.

And this is the way with out-of-control consensus. It almost always leads to poor results and – not infrequently – to disaster.

The irony? The really sad part? The dissent is always there. But it's in the background, without a safe channel. It's working, but it's undercutting decisions, destroying morale, and lowering respect for authority. And it always comes out after failure, causing anger and regrets but doing nothing for performance. Nothing ever got better by "I told you so" disagreement after the fact.

Dissent is there. We might as well put it to work for us. And to do that, we'll have to learn how to manage consensus so it doesn't get out of hand.

The Principle of Good Consensus

Luman's Law of Consensus points the way to better decisions and results by reminding us that consensus is a powerful force, for good or for bad, and that it must be managed more closely than almost any other decision-making factor.

We need to practice *consensus management*™. This important step is usually skipped, but it's actually the most important place to start.

Drucker goes on to say that "Decisions of the kind the executive has to make are not made well by acclamation. They are made well only if based on the clash of conflicting views, the dialogue between different points of view, the choice between different judgments."[22]

Notice he uses the phrase, "made *well*," not just "made."

> "THE FIRST RULE IN DECISION MAKING IS THAT ONE DOES NOT MAKE A DECISION UNLESS THERE IS DISAGREEMENT."
>
> PETER F. DRUCKER[21]

Does it take a strong leader to be willing to give up the feel-good "acclamation" and require constructive dissent in its place? Absolutely. We too easily want to hear that our thinking is stupendous and that our decisions are breathtaking. That's only natural. But it's also the way to a natural disaster.

We need to view consensus doubtfully, as more likely to be a foe than a friend. We want to be suspicious when there is no disagreeing voice, when we see decisions without doubters or directions without skeptics. Nothing is that good right out of the box. This false consensus can derive from many things: undue deference to authority, unwillingness to confront, fear of the group's displeasure, lack of commitment. But it always leads to one thing   suboptimal results.

And this means we need to take a fresh look at conflict and try to see it as a close friend. Bad conflict usually comes from bad sources, but good conflict – *constructive dissent*™ – comes from people who care, from people who are committed, from people who are more afraid of peaceful silence than of raucous disagreement.

This principle leads us to a conviction: We will only accept consensus after all *constructive dissent*™ has been mined for value. We want a sturdy, deep consensus, one that is hard-fought and comes with battle scars.

As with every important principle, we'll need what we at Luman call *PMATs*™ (practices, mechanisms, and tools) to implement it. But without this principle, cheap consensus will rule, dissent will wither away, and we'll be risking everything when the input that can save us might be hiding in an office down the hall.

The Practice of Good Consensus

How do we manage consensus so that it doesn't get out of hand? There are some key things we need to build into our leadership repertoire if we want to be successful in this optimizing practice:

Mindset. We really have to believe that consensus *can* be bad and that conflict *can* be good. It's all right to want a harmonious team as long as we define harmony as "singing different notes together" rather than "singing the same note."

Insistence. We have to *insist* on disagreement. We need to let people know that we're simply not going to move ahead until we get all questions, concerns, doubts, and differences of opinion on the table. They need to know that it's their *job* to disagree.

Forums. Especially at first, *constructive dissent*™ is hard to come by. We need to give it a home. We need to create spaces in meetings and discussions and reports so that people have structure within which they can move and disagree freely, happily, and passionately.

Risk. The risk related to disagreeing needs to be, at the very least, minimized. People need to see – and believe – that a positive difference of opinion won't lead to a negative difference in their career.

Advantages. We should think about how we can show our team that *constructive dissent*™ will work to their benefit. They have to be able to see the advantage of disagreement and that there are more and better advantages than disadvantages.

Information. People need information if they're going to be able to disagree intelligently, and they have to have the time to think about it and form their thoughts. We should especially give them information that *doesn't* support our ideas.

Once people are freely and constructively disagreeing, the path to robust, strongly supported decisions and directions is close at hand.

It will take further work to take advantage of all of this fine-looking dissonance. The goal is not to go from false consensus to honest disagreement and then to stop. The goal is to go on from the honest disagreement to *essential* agreement. *Constructive dissent*™ is only a necessary station along the way to *critical consensus*™.

It will take strong facilitation to harness all of that new creativity and energy, but once accomplished, it will pay the richest of dividends.

Here's the order, the way to progress from the unhealthy norm to a powerful place that is yours for the taking:

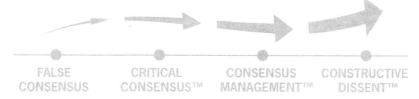

FALSE CONSENSUS → CRITICAL CONSENSUS™ → CONSENSUS MANAGEMENT™ → CONSTRUCTIVE DISSENT™

False consensus requires no further work. We quickly agree and move on. *Critical consensus*™ requires time and effort – and real leadership – to manage consensus and guide *constructive dissent*™. One is very cheap, the other quite expensive.

Great leaders see the difference, pay the price, and reap the rewards.

Take a few minutes to think about each of the practice points for good consensus. Then jot down what you can do to create the right mindset, insist on disagreement, put forums for disagreement in place, address the reasons that people might not disagree, develop incentives for disagreement, and give people the information and time to disagree effectively.

Mindset _____

_____

Insistence _____

_____

Forums _____

_____

Risk _____

_____

Advantages _____

_____

Information _____

_____

Now you can put what you've outlined above into practice on the next discussion or decision that comes your way, no matter how small the point.

After 20 years as a visual effects executive in the film and entertainment business, Deborah Giarratana has generated an astonishing list of creative achievements.

The films on which she has worked contain some of the most innovative visual effects of those 20 years: Watchmen; Spider-Man 2; I Am Legend; The Chronicles of Narnia: The Lion, the Witch and the Wardrobe; Stuart Little 2; X-Men; Star Trek: Insurrection, *and many others.*

Giarratana specializes in packaging great stories with directors and screenwriters, and in helping filmmakers to visualize and assemble their visual effects teams.

"I get so passionate and motivated working with a team and together forging ahead and reaching a goal that will bring life-changing results," she says. "That kind of dynamic has always been a part of my personality. A lot of my passion comes from finding that dynamic."

Giarratana has brought that dynamic to many of the best-known companies in the industry. Her early projects for Pacific Data Images (the company that later became DreamWorks Animation SKG®) were followed by work for James Cameron's company, Digital Domain. She has also produced new film business for Sony Pictures Imageworks, one of the leading visual effects and animation companies in the world.

"You can't fulfill your passions in life without collaborators," she says. For Giarratana, finding those creative collaborators starts with discovering your own passions.

"To find your passion, make a list of what you get excited about in life," she advises. "Find out what purpose you can serve in your world. Determine why that excites you. Those 'whys' will tell you about yourself and what motivates you. If you find a passion, I guarantee it will be tied to what motivates you."

Once you've identified your passion, Giarratana notes, finding the right collaborators becomes a much more straightforward task.

"When you find your passion, spend time with people who like the same things and have the same influences, because they'll fuel you. Don't be with people who don't understand your passion," she says. "Otherwise, it will lead to strife and confusion."

For Giarratana, collaborations between people who support and complement each other's life passions produce innovations that one person cannot produce alone.

"Your passion motivates people around you. It's infectious," she says. "Everyone will feel the reward."

TAKING THE ROAD TO THE FUTURE

Once you have the keys to a *Thinking Organization*™, you'll need a "Road to the Future."

We need to decide whether our current path is really leading to our desired destination. If it is, we need to make sure we're taking steps to get there as quickly as possible. And if not, we have to find the shortest and least damaging way to get off this dead end street and get onto the right road.

There are five main phases in taking a Road to the Future. Follow them to make sure you don't successfully arrive at the wrong place:
- Seeing the current direction clearly
- Evaluating the current direction
- Driving on the right road
- Changing directions if we're off track
- Putting up signposts to keep ourselves on the right road

Phase 1: Seeing the Current Direction Clearly

THE FIVE PHASES OF TAKING THE ROAD TO THE FUTURE
> SEEING THE CURRENT DIRECTION CLEARLY
  Evaluating the current direction
  Driving on the right road
  Changing directions if we're off track
  Putting up signposts to keep ourselves on the right road

There are a million reasons that we might not be able to see our current direction clearly.

Some of them come from outside: It isn't always easy to know what our customers or clients or partners want. Economic and industry dynamics can be shrouded in mystery. We can simply be operating off of out-of-date or irrelevant information.

Some of them can come from inside: There are lessons we've "learned" that are no longer true, people with axes to grind, unwillingness to admit that we've just wasted two years on a lousy idea.

And some can come from the fact that we are, after all, only human – full of potential to display ignorance, folly, nastiness, arrogance.

It's a lot harder to see clearly than we might think. Here are five important rules to keep in mind:

Rule 1: Clean Off Your Glasses

How much grime can accumulate on eyeglasses? I wear them, and I know it's a lot. And we can go quite a while before we think to clean them because it seems that we can still see just fine. The grime that makes it hard for

> "ALL FORMS OF DISTORTED THINKING MUST BE CORRECTED."
>
> JOHN BRADSHAW[23]

leaders to see the road includes low-priority goals, busy work, endless and pointless meetings, excessive reports, and email. You have to clear as much of this dust away as you can. You can't see the future if you can't see your nose.

Rule 2: Check Your Surroundings

Once you've cleaned your glasses, look around. Did you sign up for this? Is this where you want to be? Is this what you want to be doing? Are these the people with whom you want to travel? Is the scenery pleasant? Or are you in a wasteland? Here's the deal: If you're not passionate about where you are right now, you have serious reason to believe that you might not end up where you want to be. And thinking is going to be *really* hard.

Rule 3: Search the Horizon

If your surroundings seem about right, take a long look down the road. Can you see the payoff? Does that place look like victory? Is it worth a long drive and a lot of work? You could be in a nice place that's on the way to nowhere.

Rule 4: Ask Your Fellow Travelers

The people around you can often see that your glasses are dirty. The question is, will they be comfortable telling you? Beyond that, they can all see down the road and may have different perspectives. Two are better than one, and ten are better than two.

Rule 5: Change the Prescription

It may be that you just can't get this done without professional help. Your vision may have deteriorated. It may be hard to see how bad your vision is until an ophthalmologist shows you the world as it really is and writes you a prescription for new glasses. The "eye doctor" might be someone from another part of your organization, a colleague from another organization or industry, or an unbiased outsider. But it's worth the humility and possible cost to ask. If you can't see clearly until you get "there," even with clean glasses, you may be in for an unpleasant surprise.

VISION TEST

Take a few minutes to check in on yourself. Think about each of these important rules and write down your honest thoughts about where you are right now.

Rule 1: Clean Off Your Glasses: *What can you do to clean off the dust?*

_____

_____

_____

Rule 2: Check Your Surroundings: *What do you see? Do you like it or not?*

_____

_____

_____

Rule 3: Search the Horizon: *Where are you heading? Does that look like victory?*

_____

_____

_____

Rule 4: Ask Your Fellow Travelers: *Who can you ask this week about the team's direction?*

_____

_____

_____

Rule 5: Change the Prescription: *Who could help? What questions would you like to ask them?*

_____

_____

_____

Try to take action where you can, today.

Phase 2: Evaluating the Current Direction

THE FIVE PHASES OF TAKING THE ROAD TO THE FUTURE

Seeing the current direction clearly
> EVALUATING THE CURRENT DIRECTION
Driving on the right road
Changing directions if we're off track
Putting up signposts to keep ourselves on the right road

Whether you do it yourself, with your team, with an outsider, or with some combination, you'll want to take the time to do an honest assessment of your current direction. Pull out the stops. Nothing can be off limits. Here are some important questions to ask and answer:

1. Is our organization "the one that sets the standard"? Is it the "ultimate business competitor"? If not, why not? What could be done to change that?

2. How much time and attention are we spending on planning for the mid- and long-term future? What are we doing to prepare people for it?

3. Internally, what could make it hard for us to define the likely endpoint of our current direction?

4. What results are we happy about? Why are we getting them?

5. What are our *core excellencies*™? Are we fully exploiting them?

6. In our organization's history, to date, what is the greatest asset for future success in adding value?

7. What are the critical behaviors or actions that would be most likely to drive the creation of value?

8. What results are we unhappy about? Why are we getting them?

9. What are our *core incompetencies*™? What are we doing to reduce their impact? What should we be doing?

10. What is the greatest liability to future success in adding value?

11. What cultural/organizational factors are most inhibiting the creation of value?

12. Do we have a vision, supported by a strong mission and clear strategy, that leaders and employees are aware of and own?

13. What in the company's background or culture makes it difficult for people to think in terms of vision, mission, and long-term strategy?

14. Do we have an appropriate balance between experience/intuition about our future on the one hand and analysis/assessment on the other? How could this be improved?

15. Where do we over-analyze? Where do we under-analyze?

16. Where are we lacking the discipline to fully exploit our *core excellencies*™ or to minimize our core incompetencies?

17. Is there any useless (or relatively non-useful) work being done? Why? How could that be eliminated?

18. Are there any unresolved conflicts in thinking/culture/strategy carrying over from recent mergers, acquisitions, or other major changes? What can we do about them?

Pick your top 3 questions out of this list to begin. Once that you have a solid start on some answers, you can lay out an action plan with your team.

Phase 3: Driving on the Right Road

THE FIVE PHASES OF TAKING THE ROAD TO THE FUTURE
Seeing the current direction clearly
Evaluating the current direction
> DRIVING ON THE RIGHT ROAD
Changing directions if we're off track
Putting up signposts to keep ourselves on the right road

If you've finished your evaluation and you're reasonably sure that you are on the right road, you're ready to start driving on the Road to the Future.

Let's look at each step in detail so you can see how to do it.

Step 1: Engaging in a PitStop Protocol™

Your organization or team is like an expensive, sensitive, complicated racecar— only *more* expensive, sensitive, and complicated. If you don't take a racecar off the track on a regular basis to make sure everything's right, you're not going to win the race – and you may see the wheels come off.

The only way to go faster is to plan some time when the car isn't moving at all. Whether the *PitStop*™ lasts a day, a week, or a month depends on how much you have to evaluate.

Take some bold steps on this, right now. Make a few tentative but serious plans.

- Possible length of the *PitStop*™:

- Tentative date or dates:

- Must-have attendees:

- Like-to-have attendees:

- First-pass agenda to identify and describe the big issues:

Step 2: Selecting the "Big 3"

Rather than trying to act on 20 or 30 items, take time (As part of the *Pitstop*™ or after) to identify the 3 big "somethings" that will move your organization closer to its destination: programs, projects, initiatives—anything. What is your best guess on what they will be?

Big Item 1

Big Item 2

Big Item 3

---

* One of Luman's Signature Processes, the *PitStop Protocol*™ provides a resource for optimizing this evaluation period.

Step 3: Assigning the Best to the Best

Many organizations put their best people on their worst problems rather than on their best opportunities. Sometimes it's even worse, and we have these "winners and believers" operating in a world of random assignments – some big, some small, some unlikely to add or create value, some likely to create turnover.

You can give your best and most passionate people a shot at the best opportunities – the Big 3 you identified in Step 2. On your "guesstimated" items, how would you make your assignments?

Big Item 1

Leader:

Key Team Members:

Auxiliaries:

Goal:

Big Item 2

Leader:

Key Team Members:

Auxiliaries:

Goal:

Big Item 3

Leader:

Key Team Members:

Auxiliaries:

Goal:

Step 4: Engage in Another PitStop™

It's possible to lay out a plan that still isn't the best plan − or even a good plan. Don't do what most people do (wait until the plan obviously isn't working) before you start a re-evaluation.

Incorporate a follow-up into the original plan. Plan it in from the beginning. Depending on the scope and scale of what you're doing, you can plan it for 1 month down the road, 3 months, 6 months, or longer. But plan it in and don't let it slip away. The advantages of this re-evaluation are:
- Less likelihood of becoming delusional, because the illusions have less time to root and grow
- Greater accountability, since everyone knows a re-evaluation is coming
- Reassurance for the troops, as people know in their hearts that there is no perfect plan

Phase 4: Changing Directions If We're Off Track

THE FIVE PHASES OF TAKING THE ROAD TO THE FUTURE
  Seeing the current direction clearly
  Evaluating the current direction
  Driving on the right road
> CHANGING DIRECTIONS IF WE'RE OFF TRACK
  Putting up signposts to keep ourselves on the right road

If the evaluation turned up a different answer – that you're going nowhere fast – it's really great news in disguise. The only thing worse than having to abandon a road, retrace your steps, and find the right road? To keep going in the wrong direction!

Here are 7 things to keep in mind as you change directions:

1. ***Let people know why.*** You had some people help you evaluate the direction and come to the conclusion that you were on the wrong road. Other people will need to know how that conclusion was reached.

2. ***Define clearly what is going to change.*** It's easy to assume that everyone knows what a major change looks like. People aren't mind readers, and there is going to be enough fear and gossip and rumor to create monsters aplenty.

3. ***Let everyone know what isn't changing.*** Starting over completely is a daunting prospect. You can anchor people by letting them know all of the things that aren't going to change. This can include – as appropriate – vision, mission, components of strategy, certain products or services, aspects of brand or identity, values, and the accessibility of leaders.

4. ***Appoint a station master – or two.*** Somebody needs to have the responsibility to let you know how far and how fast to change directions. They need to relinquish their current responsibilities so they can make sure you really get on the Road to the Future.

5. ***Operate a lot of forums.*** You can't rely on the normal system of communication during a redirection time, even if it is normally effective (to make sure you're not incorrect about *that*, refer to ***The Influence Principle: Communicating and Coaching to Ignite Passion***, the eighth book in the PASSIONATE LIVES AND LEADERS SERIES). You need chances for people to express ideas, suggestions, questions, concerns, and fears, and you can't afford to wait for them to "come forward."

6. ***Help everyone define and redefine their roles.*** People need to know how they'll fit into the new world. Telling them is good. Helping them find out for themselves is even better.

7. ***Encourage courage.*** Changing directions can be a scary and demoralizing business. You can't do cheerleading only when you happen to think about it. You have to plan it and do it on a regular, consistent basis. And it has to be believable (preferably, it's believable because it's actually true). You'll also want to do lots of celebrating, not only because it helps, but because making even small changes successfully is a pretty amazing thing.

REEVALUATING THE DIRECTION

When you come to a time of redirection, take the time to address the 7 items described above. Think of a recent change and note what you might have done differently.

Let people know why.

_____

_____

_____

Define clearly what is going to change.

_____

_____

_____

Let everyone know what isn't changing.

_____

_____

_____

Appoint a station master — or two.

_____

_____

_____

Operate a lot of forums.

_____

_____

_____

Encourage courage.

_____

_____

_____

Help everyone define and redefine their roles.

_____

_____

_____

Phase 5: Putting Up Signposts to Keep Ourselves on the Right Road

Once we've found the Road to the Future, we have to understand that staying on it is far from automatic. It's a wise idea to have some signposts to let us know that we're still heading toward El Dorado – the City of Gold.

Here are our recommended signposts:

- *An 8 to10 percent drop in results, however those results are defined.* When you confirm you're on the Road to the Future and make changes to move along it faster, or when you reevaluate and find what you think is the Road to the Future, results may take a short-term hit. But like the wise equity investor who puts in a stop order to sell if the stock drops 8 to 10 percent, we should take another hard look at our investment if our results actually deteriorate beyond that threshold.

- *Increase in turnover of our best and brightest.* If our top people abandon the journey, it could be because we're on the Road to the Future, but *that* future isn't where they want to go. Or it could be their way of telling us that they don't want to be part of a train wreck. It would be a good idea to find out which of these is true.

- *A significant decline in passion and energy.* Even before people know in their minds that things are going in the wrong direction, they can often sense it in their hearts. If the fire seems to be going out, there just may be too little fuel on this desert path.

- *Unexpected negative feedback.* We can expect Wall Street or the market or customers to react skeptically to our direction, especially when we're modifying it or moving faster. But when we get negative feedback on the very points where we should most expect praise and appreciation, it's time to reconsider. It's okay to annoy people a bit, but only because we're getting *better*.

- *Good ideas that just won't work.* There are many "Wow!" ideas that fail on the most mundane of points: they can't be made to work on Planet Earth. Whatever the reason – technology or materials not available, too much money, more risk than return – no one can figure out how to make unworkable ideas work.

An Organization Built on Collective Genius

"I worked for MCI back in the days when MCI was a great place to work," says Jim Faletti, co-founder, president, and CEO of HR Insights, Ltd.

An organization can only think well, Faletti argues, if it has a fierce sense of its own reason for existing, an appropriate structure for decision making, and a healthy respect for individual differences. It's a lesson he learned in those exhilarating early days at MCI.

"I will go back, for a moment, to 1985," he says. "AT&T dominated the world. MCI was challenging AT&T, and everybody said, 'You people are nuts!' Everyone in that organization, when their feet hit the floor in the morning, knew that their mission was to beat AT&T, at every turn, every product, in the market, in advertising, in hiring people. Whether you were the receptionist or the CFO, your mission was exactly the same. Everyone knew it. Inside, of course, were all the little functional missions—the company mission, division mission—all of which are important. But the mission I am really thinking about is, Why are we here at all?"

MCI could think well about how to execute on that mission, he says, because the company's structure molded people's individual ideas and decision making into collective genius.

"MCI eventually had a lot of problems," Faletti recalls. "But back in the day when it was fighting AT&T to create the telecom industry, they very much pushed decision making down in the organization. And it allowed people both to grow personally and to have passion because a decision was their decision—to make decisions on the fly and react much quicker in the marketplace."

The decision-making criteria allowed people to invest as much creativity as they could muster. "If you were out there making 100 decisions a day and getting 75 of them right, that was much better than making 10 decisions a day and getting 9 of them right," Faletti remembers.

Having too much structure undermines thought, he says: "If you have too much structure, it kills passion. People just say, 'Why should I invest my emotion and my skills in this, when I don't have a say in its outcome anyway? I just do what I'm told.' So, people cease to innovate, they cease operating, and they check their common sense at the door when they come into work. That is too much structure. The person would never do that at home, and somehow at work, they just say, 'Oh, we just do it that way here.' They just check their common sense at the door."

A passionate organization with an appropriate structure is wired for collective brilliance. But Faletti notes that leaders need to let the innovative—and sometimes messy—process of thinking unfold.

"If you put a problem on the table and you have passionate people who are willing to invest and take the risk of having opinions and thoughts and ideas about it—if you allow that, you are going to get all those various ideas. There are a lot of leaders who think they are really consensus builders, but who 'know the answer' before it starts. I think that's phony."

"A passionate leader would be open to truly new perspectives," says Faletti. "The trick is not having chaos, and having a leadership approach that assimilates them—to create this new dish that has never been tasted before, but it is more wonderful than anything in the past."

All roads lead to a future of some kind. The *Thinking Organization*™ focuses its heart and its head to find the road that leads to a fine place – a future that will not disappoint.

"FAILURE TO ACHIEVE OBJECTIVES SHOULD BE CONSIDERED AN INDICATION THAT THE OBJECTIVE IS WRONG OR AT LEAST DEFINED WRONGLY. IF AN OBJECTIVE HAS NOT BEEN ATTAINED AFTER REPEATED TRIES, ONE HAS TO ASSUME THAT IT IS THE WRONG ONE. FAILURE TO ACHIEVE OBJECTIVES IS PRIMA FACIE REASON TO QUESTION THE VALIDITY OF THE OBJECTIVE."

PETER F. DRUCKER[24]

TIME FOR ACTION

More than ever before, we know that we have to be smart. We need clear-thinking, fact-based analysis, widespread innovation, quality decisions, and really intelligent execution. But how?

In this book, we've seen how to build the *10 Key Elements of a Thinking Organization*™ into the DNA of your organization. As Luman research shows, most leaders and organizations miss these elements, all too often in a big way. The result? Beliefs and actions based on assumptions, emotions, conflict-avoidance, phony consensus, and political turf struggles.

It doesn't have to be that way. Smart people can sum their efforts to yield smart organizations. Use the best of the organizational brain, profit from *intelligent mistakes*™, and go beyond solving problems to creating problem-driven possibilities.

You can do it. You can practice the Thinking Principle. You can build a *Thinking Organization*™.

For more on leading in a complex and contradictory world, see **The Paradox Principle: How Passionate Leaders Merge Competing Ideas,** the fourth title in the PASSIONATE LIVES & LEADERS SERIES.

FAQ

We have a lot of really smart people here. Isn't it reasonable to expect that they'll come up with good answers?

It's reasonable, but not likely. Almost nothing is more overrated than "IQ." Mental intelligence can make you smart without making you wise. On its own, it's more likely to make you arrogant than effective. Worldwide, there are many organizations that are literally filled with brilliant people, and they are often no more likely to create value than a self-trained group of people off the street.

Why the problem with early consensus? Isn't it possible for intelligent people to agree quickly on something?

Yes, but only under two conditions: 1) the answer is obvious to the most casual observer; or 2) they haven't really thought about it. Anything worth doing is worth thinking about, and if 10 reasonably intelligent people think about something worth doing, they're going to have a lot of different ideas about it. Some of those ideas will be "core," and some will be "peripheral," but the differences can be significant – and in some cases, astoundingly so. Quick agreement is a sign of intellectual surrender, not team victory.

When organizations are doing dumb things, why can't the smart people in them suggest a way out?

First of all, the smart people may in fact have suggestions for a way out; they may have the very answers needed to save the place. But if it's not a *Thinking Organization™*, how does that idea get spoken? Heard? Accepted? Implemented? But second, this is a bit like asking why a smart person can't diagnose his own illnesses: he's too close to the problem emotionally, and doesn't have the tools to do it.

Is it the norm for organizations to become progressively more unthinking?

Yes. Entropy is at work here, as it is everywhere in the universe. But it doesn't have to be so. Design can trump entropy. All that is needed is a leader committed to building a *Thinking Organization™*. That would be you.

"WHEN AN INDIVIDUAL WORKS IN A *PASSIONATE ORGANIZATION*™ THAT ENCOURAGES PASSION, THEY HAVE AN INNATE SENSE OF FREEDOM TO EXPRESS THEIR IDEAS – WITHOUT FEAR OF REPRISAL, RIDICULE. THAT FREEDOM ALLOWS INDIVIDUALS TO OFFER IDEAS THAT THEY KNOW OTHERS MAY MAKE EVEN BETTER, SO THAT THE END RESULT IS AN IDEA THAT HAS BEEN TRULY VETTED."
HELENE HARDY PIERCE, DIRECTOR OF CONTRACTOR SERVICES, GAFMC

For more on this powerful subject of passion for thinking, please see James Lucas's full-length book **Broaden the Vision and Narrow the Focus:** *Managing in a World of Paradox.*

"...ARMS A BUSINESS LEADER WITH INFORMATION ON HOW TO USE THE POWER OF PARADOXES.... MY LEADERSHIP TEAM AND I PLAN TO LEVERAGE THESE PRINCIPLES TO DEVELOP A *THINKING ORGANIZATION*™."
GLENN HARTMAN, DIRECTOR OF CUSTOMER OPERATIONS, PROCTER & GAMBLE, NORTH AMERICA

Luman International also has an in-depth assessment, the Thinking Quotient™, which will provide you tremendous insight into your organization's Thinking DNA, Infrastructure, Leadership, People, and Transformation/Adaptive Capacity.

We offer a full-day course, "Building a Thinking Organization," and a number of keynotes or short presentations on the topic, including "Releasing the Dynamic of Collective Thought™."

We can assist you on several aspects of designing and building a thinking organization with our Signature Processes, including "Using the Strategic Planning Framework™" and "Executing Strategy."

For more information, please visit lumaninternational.com.

Endnotes

1. *Accessed 9 September 2008. Available: http://www.quoteworld.org/quotes/2946.*

2. *In the Luman course* Building a Thinking Organization™™, *we cover these questions in some detail.*

3. *In the Luman course* Building a Thinking Organization™, *we cover these statements in some detail.*

4. *In the Luman course* Building a Thinking Organization™, *we cover 7 of these "Methods of Inquiry" in some detail.*

5. *Shapiro, Fred R.* The Yale Book of Quotations. *New Haven: Yale University Press, 2006.*

6. *Accessed 17 October 2008. Available: http://www.brainyquote.com/quotes/authors/d/dan_quisenberry.html.*

7. *Luman International has an in-depth assessment, the* Thinking Quotient™, *to determine an organization's level of* Thinking Capital™ *to highlight gaps and to provide direction for improvement.*

8. *Barry, Dave.* Dave Barry Turns 50. *"25 Things I Have Learned in 50 Years." New York: The Ballantine Publishing Group, 1998.*

9. *Accessed 27 September 2008. Available: http://www.goodreads.com/quotes/show/12243.*

10. *Accessed 14 October 2008. Available: http://www.quotationspage.com/quote/29606.html.*

11. *Quoted in "Letters."* Time. *16 January 2007. Accessed 14 September 2008. Available: http://www.time.com/time/magazine/article/0,9171,1578169,00.html.*

12. Oxford English Reference Dictionary, *Revised Second Edition. Oxford: Oxford University Press, 2003.*

13. *Quoted in "Thoughts on the Business Life."* Forbes *Nov. 8, 1982: 280.*

14. *James R. Lucas,* Broaden the Vision and Narrow the Focus: Managing in a World of Paradox. *Westport, CT: Praeger Publishers, 2006.*

15. *Quoted in Ralph Keyes,* The Quote Verifier: Who Said What, Where, and When. *New York: Macmillan, 2006.*

16. *Accessed 14 October 2008. Available: http://www.quotationspage.com/quote/32863.html.*

17. *Accessed 9 September 2008. Available: http://quotationsbook.com/quote/16701/.*

18. *Accessed 12 November 2008. Available: http://www.quotationspage.com/quote/26189.html.*

19. *For more on how to build* powersharing™ *into your culture, see Jim's book* Balance of Power: Fueling Employee Power without Relinquishing Your Own. *Kansas City, MO: Quintessential Books, 2002.*

20. *Quoted in* Simpson's Contemporary Quotations, *compiled by James B. Simpson. Boston: Houghton Mifflin Company, 1988.*

21. *Drucker, Peter F.* The Essential Drucker: The Best of Sixty Years of Peter Drucker's Essential Writngs on Management. *New York: HarperCollins, 2003.*

22. Ibid.

23. *Accessed 8 September 2008. Available: http://thinkexist.com/quotation/it-s_essential_to_tell_the_truth_at_all_times/261588.html*

24. *Drucker, Peter F.* Innovation and Entrepreneurship. *New York: HarperCollins, 2006.*

JAMES R. LUCAS

James R. Lucas is a recognized authority on leadership and cultural design. He is a groundbreaking author and thought leader, provocative speaker, and experienced consultant on these crucial topics.

Jim is President and CEO of Luman International, an organization which he founded in 1983. This firm is dedicated to Developing Passionate, Thinking, Pure-Performance Organizations™ and their leaders, people, and teams.

Clients are from sectors as diverse as health care, pharmaceuticals, medical devices, financial services, accounting, energy, chemicals, forest and paper products, transportation, computer hardware, diversified manufacturing, consumer products, diversified business services, construction, state government, and federal government. They range from Fortune 1000 public companies and private for-profit organizations to not-for-profits and government agencies.

Jim has written numerous curricula for business and leadership seminars, as well as many essays and articles. In addition to the PASSIONATE LIVES AND LEADERS series, he is the author of five other landmark books on leadership and organizational development:

- High-Performance Ethics: *10 Timeless Principles for Next Generation Leadership*
- Broaden the Vision and Narrow the Focus: *Managing in a World of Paradox*
- The Passionate Organization: *Igniting the Fire of Employee Commitment*
- Balance of Power: *Fueling Employee Power without Relinquishing Your Own*
- Fatal Illusions: *Shredding a Dozen Unrealities That Can Keep Your Organization from Success*

Prior to founding Luman International, Jim was President of EMCI, a high-tech design and manufacturer of aerospace systems and medical devices. Before that, he held managerial and executive positions at Hallmark Cards, VF Corporation, and Black & Veatch Consulting Engineers.

Jim is an award-winning senior faculty member of the American Management Association, where he served for several years as a charter member of the Faculty Advisory Council. He taught its premier course, The Course for Presidents (in which he was and is the highest-rated faculty member), and is the overall highest-rated faculty member in the history of the AMA. He is also a frequent presenter at the Center for Leadership & Executive Development. Jim has an extensive speaking schedule, in which he addresses topics from his books and research, and has been interviewed frequently on radio and television.

Jim received his education in leadership, business, economics, and engineering at the University of Missouri (Columbia and Rolla), where he received his Ph.D. (h.c.). He has also taught at Rockhurst University. Jim is past president of the Academy of Engineering Management, a member of the American Society for Training and Development, a member of the American Society of Engineering Management, a senior member of the Society of Manufacturing Engineers, and a registered professional engineer in Missouri and Kansas.

Jim has been honored with continuous listings in *Who's Who in America* (1999-2009), *Who's Who in the World* (1989-2008), and *Who's Who in Finance & Industry* (1989-2009).

PHIL HOTSENPILLER

Phil Hotsenpiller is an executive coach who brings his wealth of professional experience, creativity, and spiritual insight to passionate leaders around the world.

Phil is the founder and President of New York Executive Coaching Group, a firm that has assisted Presidents, CEOs, and other professionals to achieve breakthrough results in their professional and personal lives. His clients are a diverse and accomplished array of leaders in many sectors: arts and entertainment, finance and industry, and religious and not-for-profit.

Phil is also the Executive Director of the not-for-profit International Freedom (IF). IF is working with its partners to build 200 education centers for Dalit children and 200 vocational training centers for Dalit women throughout India. Using the power of documentary film, International Freedom also seeks to raise awareness among Hollywood "influencers" of the plight of the Dalit people in order to bring about lasting change. IF's acclaimed documentary, DELETES, was selected to compete in the Artivist Film Festival and the HollyShorts Film Festival, where it earned the Audience Choice Award. In addition, IF has recruited more than 1000 volunteers to serve urban Los Angeles, feeding the homeless and creating after-school programs and health clinics.

Throughout his career, Phil has worked extensively on issues at the nexus of leadership, artistry, and spirituality. Previously, he served as adjunct professor in a division of Southern Theological Seminary and Union Theological Seminary. He has spoken on leadership and theology throughout Mexico, Brazil, Paraguay, El Salvador, Honduras, Guatemala, Romania, Yugoslavia, and France, working with the European Team of Christian Associates International in the area of leadership development. He was one of 25 selected to serve on the Pastors Task Force for the War on Drugs organized by former U.S. "drug czar" William Bennett. Phil also founded *One Purpose*, a weekly television show on WSFJ-TV and a daily radio broadcast on WRFD radio.

Phil continues to address these issues, facilitating a weekly group of 100 prominent actors and young leaders in the Hollywood entertainment industry. With bestselling graphic novel artist/illustrator Rob Liefield, Phil is a founding partner of 12 Gates Productions, an entertainment company producing a full line of graphic novels, lithographs, DVDs, feature-length films, and video games. He currently serves as Teaching Pastor at Yorba Linda Friends Church in Southern California; YLFC was recently honored as one of the 100-fastest growing churches in the United States. As a leader of discovery trips to Europe, Phil teaches European history, art, philosophy, religion, and culture in Geneva, Amsterdam, and Aix-en-Provence. These trips provide participants with an understanding of different cultures and build bridges between passionate people around the world.

Phil received his education in history, religion, political science, and English literature at Southwest Baptist University. He earned his Master of Divinity from New Orleans Baptist Theological Seminary and completed postgraduate studies at Christ Church College, Oxford University.

Phil is married to Tammy Hotsenpiller, author of *A Taste of Humanity* (2009) and co-founder and designer of Humanity™ for All, LLC, a cutting-edge clothing line noted for its original art with an urban flair and its strong links with dozens of social justice organizations. Songwriter Tye-V (Nycolia Turman) is writing lyrics for an upcoming Humanity™ album.

THE PASSIONATE LIVES & LEADERS SERIES

Book 1 - The Passion Principle: *Designing a Passionate Organization*
Book 2 - The Attraction Principle: *Finding, Keeping and Teaming Passionate People*
Book 3 - The Thinking Principle: *Using Passion to Innovate and Create Value*
Book 4 - The Paradox Principle: *How Passionate Leaders Merge Competing Ideas*
Book 5 - The Performance Principle: *Delivering Results through the Power of Passion*
Book 6 - The Confidence Principle: *Discovering Your Life's Passion and a Place to Live It*
Book 7 - The Reality Principle: *Exploiting Change and Crisis with Courage and Passion*
Book 8 - The Influence Principle: *Communicating and Coaching to Ignite Passion*

You and every member of your organization will be inspired by this 8-book series, in which real-world leaders share their experiences in building passionate teams and organizations. Read how the ultimate competitive advantage is harnessing the passion that leads to outstanding performance!

For more about THE PASSIONATE LIVES AND LEADERS SERIES,
visit www.livesandleaders.com.

To order, or to learn more about volume discounts for individual books and sets, visit Quintessential Books at www.quintessentialbooks.com.

To learn more about implementing these principles, visit Luman International at www.lumaninternational.com.

Quintessential Books

READ BOLDLY. THINK DEEPLY. LIVE PASSIONATELY.
www.quintessentialbooks.com